COVERT CAREERS
Jobs You Can't Talk About

INSIDE
INTERPOL

LOUISE SPILSBURY

LUCENT
P R E S S

Published in 2019 by
Lucent Press, an Imprint of Greenhaven Publishing, LLC
353 3rd Avenue
Suite 255
New York, NY 10010

Produced for Lucent by Calcium
Designers: Paul Myerscough and Jeni Child
Picture researcher: Rachel Blount
Editors: Sarah Eason and Jennifer Sanderson

Picture credits: Cover: Shutterstock: Gorodenkoff; Inside: Flickr: National Police of Colombia:
p. 39; ©INTERPOL: pp. 5, 16–17t, 18, 21; Shutterstock: Volodymyr Burdiak: p. 14; Chombosan:
p. 9; Create jobs 51: p. 37; David M G: p. 36; Frans Delian: pp. 28–29t, 29b; Dencg: p. 24;
Paravyan Eduard: pp. 3, 11; Gorodenkoff: p. 27; Hafakot: p. 42; Matej Kastelic: p. 16b; Kentoh:
p. 20; Gorodenkoff/Shutterstock.com: p. 19; Artem Oleshko: p. 34; Photographee.eu: p. 41;
Pressmaster: p. 38; Sdecoret: p. 23; Structuresxx: p. 13; Tommaso79: p. 26; Robert Paul Van Beets:
p. 43; Vectorsector: p. 35; Welcomia: p. 15; Katherine Welles: p. 40; HUANG Zheng: pp. 7, 44–45;
Wikimedia Commons: Matt Aronoff/NIST: p. 22; Bluuurgh: p. 25; Michael Büker: p. 30;
European Communities: p. 6; Victor Grigas: p. 10; Jordiferrer: pp. 32, 33; Manfred Kopka: p. 31;
Mriya: p. 4; Edvard Munch: p. 12; National Police of Colombia: p. 8.

Cataloging-in-Publication Data

Names: Spilsbury, Louise.
Title: Inside Interpol / Louise Spilsbury.
Description: New York : Lucent Press, 2019. | Series: Covert careers: jobs you can't talk about |
Includes glossary and index.
Identifiers: ISBN 9781534566323 (pbk.) | ISBN 9781534566330 (library bound) |
ISBN 9781534566347 (ebook)
Subjects: LCSH: International Criminal Police Organization--Juvenile literature. |
Law enforcement--International cooperation--Juvenile literature. |
Criminal investigation--International cooperation--Juvenile literature.
Classification: LCC HV7240.I25 S65 2019 | DDC 363.206'01--dc23

Printed in the United States of America

CPSIA compliance information: Batch BW19KL: For further information, contact Greenhaven
Publishing, LLC, New York, New York, at 1-844-317-7404.

Please visit our website, www.greenhavenpublishing.com. For a free color catalog of all our
high-quality books, call toll free 1-844-317-7404 or fax 1-844-317-7405.

CONTENTS

CHAPTER 1

WHAT IS INTERPOL?

Interpol is an abbreviation for the International Criminal Police Organization. It is the largest police organization in the world. Interpol brings together a network of police forces from 192 countries all over the world. It enables police across the globe to work together to solve crimes that cross borders, making the world a safer place.

Crossing Borders

In the past, when transportation options were limited, a person would commit a crime in one place and they would stay in that region. Today, it is much easier to be anywhere in the world within 24 hours. Imagine that a criminal commits a crime, such as a robbery, in the United Kingdom (UK) and then flees from that country and goes to the United States. Or, what if they commit crimes in several countries and keep moving on? How do the police working in the UK find the criminal? This is where Interpol can help solve the crime and help police catch the criminal.

Interpol works with police forces of all kinds from around the world.

Technology and Crimes

Today, the use of computers and the Internet makes crime international. For example, a criminal using a computer on one side of the world can hack into a person's bank accounts across the globe without the hacker even leaving their house. Criminals from around the world can also connect with others via the Internet to organize crimes using the World Wide Web. Interpol investigates a variety of crimes, including terrorism, organized crime, illegal drug production and trafficking, people and weapons smuggling, money laundering, financial crime, high-tech crime, and political corruption.

Interpol officers seize fake goods. The fake goods' packaging is often so convincing that consumers do not realize that they are buying illicit products.

Inside Interpol

Interpol is a highly respected international organization with high standards. Anyone working for Interpol is expected to show respect for and commitment to universal human rights and cultural diversity. That means that they have to treat colleagues from a variety of backgrounds, cultures, and experiences with dignity and respect.

The Idea for Interpol

The idea of Interpol was discussed in 1914 at the First International Criminal Police Congress in Monaco. At this congress, police officers and lawyers from 24 different countries met to talk about arrest procedures, identification techniques, centralized international criminal records, and methods of sending criminals who cross borders back to the country from which they came or where they committed a crime. However, the International Criminal Police Commission (ICPC) was not started until nine years later, in 1923. Since the creation of the organization was set in motion by Dr. Johannes Schober, who was president of the Vienna Police, its first headquarters were in Vienna, Austria.

The ICPC in World War II

During World War II, Nazi Germany took control of Austria. The ICPC also came under Nazi control, and its headquarters were moved to Berlin, Germany. The ICPC was intended to be independent of any single country and run by representatives from different countries who were elected to their posts. Under Adolf Hitler, however, the ICPC had only Nazi leaders doing work that benefited only Germany. After the war ended, Belgium instigated the rebuilding of the organization with its original structure from a new headquarters in Paris, France. At this time, "INTERPOL" was chosen as the organization's telegraphic address.

All Interpol officers are issued an identity (ID) card for travel.

Interpol Today

In 1956, the organization agreed on a modern set of rules and changed its name to the International Criminal Police Organization INTERPOL, shortened to ICPO–INTERPOL or just INTERPOL. The organization became totally independent by collecting payments from all member countries as its main source of funding. In 1989, Interpol moved to its present headquarters in Lyon, France.

The General Secretariat of Interpol operates 24 hours a day, 365 days a year at its headquarters in Lyon, France.

The Interpol Emblem

The Interpol emblem, which has been used since 1950, has the following symbols:

- The image of the globe shows that Interpol's activities are worldwide.
- Olive branches on either side of the globe are symbols of peace.
- An upright sword behind the globe is a symbol of police action.
- The scales below the olive branches symbolize justice.

Connecting Police

Today, Interpol connects police forces in 192 countries around the world and uses modern technology to help it tackle the growing challenges of fighting crime. Interpol works to ensure that police forces around the world have the tools and information they need to do their jobs. It has a large database of criminals and crimes, which includes information such as illegal drugs and lost and stolen passports and visas. Police in member countries use Interpol's help and information to carry out investigations.

Interpol officers update their criminal database, so that police in member countries can access the latest information to help them in their investigations.

Governing Interpol

Interpol is run by the General Assembly and Executive Committee. The General Assembly is a group of people who are appointed by each member country to meet every year to discuss and make important decisions about Interpol, such as how countries work together, funding, activities, resources, and programs. The Executive Committee is chosen by the General Assembly. It is led by a different president every four years. The president and committee make sure that Interpol follows the General Assembly's decisions.

Day-to-Day Decisions

The day-to-day running of Interpol is carried out by the General Secretariat and National Central Bureaus (NCBs). The General Secretariat is run by the Secretary General and based at Interpol headquarters in Lyon, France. The Secretariat has seven regional bureaus around the world, along with Special Representatives at the African Union (Addis Ababa), the European Union (Brussels), and the United Nations (New York). There is an NCB in each Interpol member country. Interpol can contact each of these special offices to get information or for any other action. In turn, each NCB can contact Interpol or the police force of another member country to ask for any assistance.

NCBs use a secure, high-speed computer network to contact each other at any time.

Inside Interpol

The skilled police officers who work in NCBs contribute to Interpol's criminal databases and cooperate together in investigations, operations, and arrests that cross international borders. It is vital that these officers are good at communicating and working with other people on a variety of crimes.

9

INTERPOL IN ACTION

Interpol works to prevent and investigate a wide range of crimes around the world by sharing expertise, information, technical tools, and resources, and by coordinating important international investigations.

Terrorism

Terrorism is the use of violence or the threat of violence, such as murder and bombing, to influence people or force a government to do something. Terrorist acts, such as the 9/11 attacks in the United States, cause terrible destruction and fear. One way in which Interpol works to help prevent terrorist acts is by storing and analyzing information about suspects and their activities, and sharing this information with member countries and other international groups. Interpol has set up a special group, the Counter-Terrorism Fusion Centre (CTF), to investigate how terrorist groups are funded and run, their motives, and how they find, recruit, and train new terrorists.

Mourners left these mementoes to remember those killed in a terrorist attack in Nice, France, in 2016.

Interpol officers examine bills and other suspicious currency to see if they are counterfeit, or fake.

Financial Crime and Corruption

Financial crimes include making counterfeit money and money laundering. Money laundering is when criminals hide money made by crime in a cash-based business such as a restaurant, or by putting it in many different bank accounts. Financial crimes also include stealing bank cards or making fake ones and things such as phishing, in which fake emails are sent to trick people into handing over money.

Corruption is illegal and dishonest behavior by people in business or politics for their own personal gain, for example, taking bribes. Both corruption and financial crime encourage organized criminal activities, including terrorism, because they give criminals funds to pay for their illegal activities. Criminals are then able to commit crimes because corrupt public officials turn a blind eye to their activities.

Pirates at Sea

Interpol also helps police officers catch modern-day pirates who attack ships at sea, kidnap those on board, and demand high ransom payments for their safe return. Interpol is helping train police in regions where this is common, and it is developing a global database on maritime piracy, to collect, analyze, and share relevant information.

Trafficking

Trafficking means to deal or trade in something illegal. Trafficking usually means that goods are transported and sold in different countries, so most trafficking crimes are international by their very nature. Interpol is involved in helping to solve a variety of trafficking crimes.

Interpol's database of stolen works of art helps law enforcement agencies across the world trace stolen paintings and other works of art.

Trafficking Crimes:

- Drugs: Illegal drugs such as marijuana, cocaine, and heroin are smuggled from countries where they are produced and sold across the world.
- Firearms: The illegal trafficking of firearms results in weapons being in the hands of dangerous criminals. Trafficked firearms have been used in recent global terrorist activities.
- Vehicles: Vehicles are stolen to sell but are also trafficked to fund other crimes. They can be used to transport bombs or carry out other crimes.
- Illicit goods: The trafficking of fake or counterfeit products means that dangerous and substandard goods are sold on the market.
- Works of art: Paintings, sculptures, and other works of art (often of great historical value) are stolen from the country where they belong and sold abroad illegally.

Human Trafficking

Trafficking in human beings is a form of modern-day slavery. People are deceived or forced into leaving their homes and trafficked between countries and regions, to be sold, for example, as servants working for little or no money. They are robbed of their freedom and choice, and many are beaten and treated very cruelly.

Crimes Against Children

Children are also trafficked and sold across borders. Other crimes against children include sexual abuse, for example, where criminals contact children either directly or via chat rooms and social networking sites in order to abuse them, or by taking and sharing inappropriate images of them. Another crime is sex tourism, in which someone travels to poorer countries in order to abuse children there.

Interpol works to stop human trafficking and to protect the victims of this crime.

Sports Crimes

Crimes such as match fixing, illegal gambling, and doping affect **sports** globally. For example, team managers or coaches may be bribed to make sure their team loses, so that criminals can make money betting on that outcome. Crimes in sports cross international borders and generate huge profits. One way Interpol helps is by conducting investigations alongside organizations such as the International Olympic Committee (IOC) to dismantle the networks behind crimes in sports.

Environmental Crime

Environmental crime includes the illegal trade in wild plants and animals. It also includes polluting wild areas, such as rivers, by disposing of waste and hazardous substances. A lot of environmental crime is carried out by organized criminal networks that use the same routes to smuggle wildlife as they do to smuggle other goods. Interpol intelligence is used to lead global and regional missions to dismantle the criminal networks behind these crimes.

Interpol uses global operations to keep people from trading in animal parts, such as ivory from elephant tusks.

War Crimes

War crimes include torture, the forced removal of a group of people from their home, and genocide, which is the deliberate killing of people from a particular nation or ethnic group. Interpol helps nations prevent, investigate, and prosecute these crimes. For example, Interpol trains local police working on war crime cases in the most up-to-date investigative skills in areas such as the collection and processing of evidence related to **mass** murder.

Cybercrime

Cybercrime is when criminals use the Internet to commit crimes. Some cybercriminals develop and use software to access important data that belongs to a business or country. Other cybercriminals use the Internet to carry out more traditional crimes, such as theft. Cybercrime costs countries billions of dollars and is often committed by international networks of cybercriminals. One of the ways Interpol helps is by using digital forensics. This is the recovery and investigation of material found in digital devices.

Wanted!

Interpol posts photographs and details of people who have committed war crimes, so that the general public can be on the lookout for these criminals. People can tell Interpol which country the criminal has been seen in, so Interpol can tell police in that country to track them down.

Cybercrime is a fast-growing area of crime and one that has no borders.

CHAPTER 3

THE INTERPOL TEAM

In order to tackle the wide and complex range of international crimes that Interpol deals with, the organization needs a team of talented individuals working in different roles. Unlike most other law enforcement agencies, Interpol officers do not usually arrest criminals themselves. Most officers work in offices, not in the field, collecting and analyzing information to help the law enforcement agencies of Interpol member countries.

The Team at the Command and Coordination Centre

The Command and Coordination Centre (CCC) is Interpol's main operations room. Officers here are the first point of contact for police forces from any member country that needs Interpol's help to solve a crime. The CCC is based at the General Secretariat in Lyon, France. There are two other operations rooms: one in Buenos Aires, Argentina, and another in Singapore, which is part of the Interpol Global Complex for Innovation (IGCI). Operations rooms have to be able and ready to support international police in real time, so they are open 24 hours a day, every day of the year.

Collecting and analyzing information is a vital part of Interpol's work.

The teams working in operations rooms support Interpol officers in the field.

Working at the CCC

The main activities of Interpol officers at the CCC include:

- Sifting through communications and messages that come in to decide which are most important and which should take priority
- Replying to urgent requests by doing instant checks on all Interpol databases
- Assessing potential threats and ensuring that all resources are ready and available if needed
- Coordinating the exchange of intelligence and information for important operations
- Issuing global or regional alerts and publishing notices of potential threats and wanted criminals
- Managing serious incidents, such as terror attacks, and organizing and providing response teams to assist at those incidents
- Organizing and providing response teams to help national police with security arrangements at major international events that attract large crowds

Inside Interpol

The CCC offers 24-hour support for officers in NCBs in member countries. CCC staff members of various nationalities are fluent in several different languages. To get a job with Interpol, people need to have knowledge of at least one of the organization's four official languages: Arabic, English, French, and Spanish.

Response Teams

At the request of member countries, Interpol can provide teams of specially trained officers to help national police forces cope with major incidents. The teams are made up of experts in relevant fields, and they give the local police forces their expertise in investigative support, for example, with rapid access to fingerprint, DNA, digital forensic, and firearms databases.

Border Task Forces

Members of the Integrated Border Management Task Force (IBMTF) work on international border security activities. Border controls are controls on the movement of people, animals, and goods into and out of a country. IBMTF officers work at air, land, and sea border points, and they help local law enforcement officers access Interpol databases to catch criminals. Border task forces also train staff to improve border controls.

The IBMTF centralizes Interpol's border security efforts.

Incident Response Teams

Incident response teams (IRTs) are made up of expert Interpol police and support staff. They are sent out after a natural disaster, such as a flood or earthquake, or a major crime, such as a terror attack. IRTs travel to the disaster zone and assist with victim identification, suspect identification, and sharing information to other nations' law enforcement agencies.

Interpol provides security support for events such as the FIFA World Cup opening celebration.

Major Events Support Teams

Interpol Major Events Support Teams (IMESTs) help plan and prepare, coordinate, and carry out security arrangements for major events, such as United Nations conferences and the FIFA World Cup. They access fingerprints, photos, wanted person notices, and data relating to stolen and lost travel documents and stolen vehicles that might help identify individuals who want to disrupt an event to gain attention for their cause or for criminal gain.

Inside Interpol

In total, there can be 650 people from up to 90 different countries working at any one time at the Interpol General Secretariat, its regional bureaus, and liaison offices.

Analyzing computers to discover or recover data to do with crime can be a painstaking task.

Criminal Intelligence Analysis

Criminal intelligence analysts study data relating to criminals, suspects, and incidents, and trends and other issues to do with crime. They collect and assess data and write reports about the connections between different crimes in different places.

Interpol Analysts

Operational analysts work on particular operations. This might be an arrest, a seizure of goods or money gained from criminal activities, or the breaking up of a criminal group. Operational analysts find information that links suspects to specific crimes, and they prepare profiles of known or suspected criminals. Strategic analysts work on providing early warnings of threats to help senior decision makers prepare their organizations to deal with future criminal issues. This might include increasing training in a particular crime-fighting technique. Strategic analysts study crime trends and patterns, emerging threats, and the potential impact of things like improvements in technology, demographics, or economics on crime.

Fugitive Investigation Officers

Fugitives are criminals who are running away from the law, perhaps because they have fled while on bail or escaped from prison. Fugitives often travel between countries using stolen or fake travel documents and pay for their escape by committing more crimes. Interpol helps locate and arrest fugitives who cross international boundaries by providing investigative support in international fugitive investigations, conducting specific operations to catch particular groups of fugitives, and coordinating international cooperation in fugitive investigations. Interpol also helps find people who are wanted for genocide and war crimes.

Working in Forensics

Some Interpol officers work on maintaining Interpol's databases of fingerprints, DNA profiles, and facial images, allowing police around the world to make connections between criminals and crime scenes. Some forensics experts also provide training to the police in member countries, to give those officers the knowledge and skills they need to assess, preserve, and share evidence in the best way possible.

Inside Interpol

Analysts are not always in the office. Sometimes, they travel to train investigation and intelligence police officers in other regions or member countries to improve their skills in, for example, counterterrorism or human trafficking. This means that analysts not only require detective skills but also teaching and training skills.

Interpol's DNA database was created in 2002.

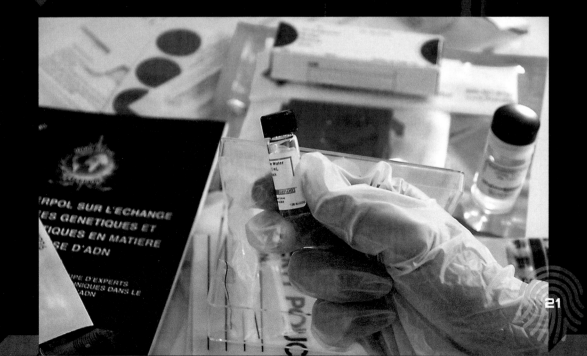

CHAPTER 4

TECHNIQUES AND TOOLS

Interpol relies on a system of communications, technologies, and databases to carry out its work effectively and to help track criminals and their activities across international borders.

The Power of Databases

Interpol has a number of databases covering all types of evidence, from fingerprints to stolen passports and DNA profiles. When DNA samples are collected at a crime scene, for example, from hair or skin cells left by a criminal, the sample is analyzed, and a DNA profile is created. Interpol keeps these profiles in its database, so that when DNA is found at another crime scene, it can be compared to those in the database to find person-to-scene, scene-to-scene, or person-to-person matches where no previous connection was known.

Law enforcement officers can take fingerprints using an electronic device, or they can take them manually using ink and paper, then scan them to save the data electronically to the Interpol database.

How I-24/7 Works

When police officers find fingerprints, they run them against databases to catch the criminal. Very often they use I-24/7. I-24/7 is Interpol's highly secure internal computer network, which can be used only by the police forces of member countries. It allows them to search any of Interpol's international criminal databases. For example, if police forces have an image or sketch of a suspect they know has escaped to another country, they can run it through Interpol's facial recognition service. This contains more than 44,000 images of people from 137 countries. By running the image through Interpol software, police forces across the globe can identify fugitives and missing persons, and make connections between criminals and crime scenes.

Satellite Links

Satellite technology is vital to Interpol's work. For example, each NCB is connected to the I-24/7 network system by satellite. The system allows contact with other countries around the clock, 24/7!

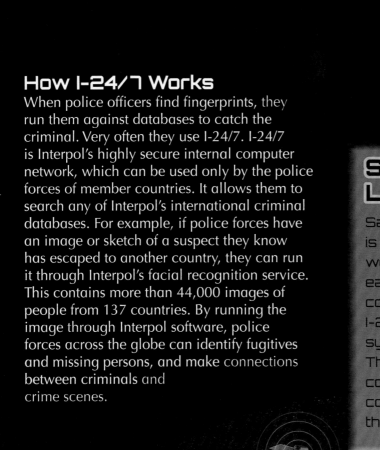

Satellites above Earth can receive and transmit data around the planet instantly.

Alerts and Notices

One of Interpol's most powerful tools in solving international crimes is the system of alerts, known as notices, that they issue. A notice is a type of message that is sent to all member countries worldwide. Most notices alert police agencies about a particular situation or suspect and include as much information as possible to help police deal with an investigation, such as finding a dangerous person or identifying a body. Notices each have a different color, depending on their use.

Notice Colors:

- Orange: to warn of an event, person, object, or process that represents an imminent threat and danger to persons or property
- Black: to seek information on unidentified bodies
- Yellow: to locate a missing person or to identify a person unable to identify themself
- Green: to warn about a person's criminal activities, if that person is considered to be a possible threat to public safety
- Blue: to locate, identify, or obtain information on a person of interest in a criminal investigation
- Red: to seek the location and arrest of a person wanted by the law with a view to their extradition
- Purple: to provide information on procedures, objects, devices, or hiding places used by criminals

ALERT

Interpol alerts are one of the main ways Interpol helps international police work together.

How Do Notices Work?

Imagine that a criminal has escaped from one country and is on the run. Police officers in the member country—where the fugitive escaped from jail—request a red notice from Interpol. They do this by contacting their NCB and providing that bureau with identification details and any information that the courts have about the wanted person. Interpol officers check the case, and the General Secretariat publishes the notice. The red notice alerts police around the world and gives border officials the information they need to spot the fugitive, making it difficult for the fugitive to travel. Countries share critical information linked to the ongoing investigation through Interpol, until eventually, the fugitive is located, arrested by local police, and sent back to the country from which they escaped. There, the criminal will stand trial.

Interpol sends out alerts and warnings about terrorists, dangerous criminals, and weapons threats to police in member countries.

A New Interpol Notice

A new Interpol United Nations (UN) Security Council special notice was created in 2005. It informs member countries that an individual or group, such as the Taliban, is subject to UN sanctions.

Digital Forensics in Action

Digital forensics is a branch of forensic science that covers the recovery and investigation of material found in digital devices, often in relation to computer crime. The IGCI in Singapore opened in 2014 and is a center of excellence for digital forensics technology. Experts in cybercrime investigation support research and development in the area of digital crime, and digital security personnel from Interpol member countries work here in the Digital Forensics Lab and the Cyber Fusion Centre.

Digital Forensics Lab

Experts in the Digital Forensics Lab can help police in member countries preserve, extract, analyze, and understand data from mobile devices, such as laptop computers, cell phones, and hard drives. Sometimes, experts from the lab are sent into the field with specialist digital forensics equipment. Member countries may also send devices to the lab to be analyzed. The experts use highly specialized digital forensics techniques and technologies to help recover data, decode encrypted contents, and get through password locks on computers and mobile devices. They also have the tools to recover data from devices that have been physically damaged in attempts by criminals to destroy evidence.

Interpol engineers repair and fix broken hard drives, so data can be recovered from them.

Cyber Fusion Centre

Inside the Cyber Fusion Centre, there are huge screens on the walls in front of Interpol officers' workstations. The screens display the latest information on cyberthreats from all over the world, such as malware outbreaks. Malware is software that is specifically designed to disrupt, damage, or gain unauthorized access to a computer system. The Fusion Centre uses the latest technology to monitor criminal Internet activities in real time, so they can provide member agencies with information they need to take action. They also research and test new technologies and the way they are used by criminals, so that they stay one step ahead of the international criminals who specialize in cybercrime.

High-tech facilities like the Cyber Fusion Centre use the latest computer technology.

Inside Interpol

Workers at the IGCI in Singapore come from law enforcement agencies within Interpol member countries, but they also come from banks, private industries, and universities. Interpol values computing and technological expertise from any industry, so people do not have to be directly connected with Interpol to apply for a job here.

CHAPTER 5

FAMOUS INTERPOL CASES

Interpol has been involved in many famous incidents and investigations, and the arrest of some notorious and dangerous criminals. The organization has also done very important work after natural disasters.

Tsunami 2004

On December 26, 2004, a powerful undersea earthquake off the coast of the Indonesian island of Sumatra set off a devastating series of tsunami waves in the Indian Ocean. The earthquake struck at 8:00 a.m. Within two hours, tsunami waves hit the eastern coasts of India and Sri Lanka about 750 miles (1,200 km) away. Five hours after that, tsunami waves hit the coast of East Africa. The tsunami killed more than 230,000 people in 12 countries, with Indonesia, Sri Lanka, India, the Maldives, and Thailand suffering the worst damage.

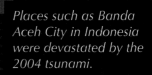

Places such as Banda Aceh City in Indonesia were devastated by the 2004 tsunami.

How Interpol Helped

When any natural disaster occurs, it is important to identify bodies. This allows families of the deceased to choose a grave or resting place for their loved ones, and to be able to know for certain where they were and what happened to them. After the 2004 tsunami, Interpol created a support group of Interpol staff and officials from member countries to help teams identify the victims of the tsunami. Interpol set up a centralized storage point in affected countries for DNA profiles, fingerprints, and other victim identification data, and national processes for matching samples to unidentified victims' bodies.

Disaster Victim Identification Guide

Interpol produces a regularly updated disaster victim identification guide. It provides guidelines for member countries in ways of identifying victims of disasters. It tells them how to set up a disaster victim identification team and how to manage disaster victim identification operations.

The guidelines advise on major issues of victim identification, such as the need for temporary sites to store bodies equipped with refrigerated containers, mobile forensic laboratories, and work facilities.

Many children lost their parents and were left orphaned by the tsunami.

The Hunt for Milan Lukic

The story of the hunt and capture of Milan Lukic is an Interpol success story that demonstrates the critical role the organization's NCBs play in global police cooperation. In the 1990s, there was a civil war between different ethnic groups in the countries that were once part of Yugoslavia. During the war, Serbian forces engaged in the genocide of Bosnian Muslims. Milan Lukic was one of the most notorious Serbian mass murderers and army chiefs from the war in Bosnia.

On the Run

Lukic was a violent leader who lived near the Muslim-majority town of Višegrad, near the border with Serbia. He led a military group known as the White Eagles. The White Eagles marched Muslims from Višegrad into houses that were then burned down, with Lukic waiting outside to shoot any men, women, or children who tried to escape. Other victims were lined up on a bridge or the banks of the Drina River and shot, their bodies dumped in the river. Women and girls were held in camps where they were abused. After the war ended, Lukic went on the run in Latin America.

There are the many gravestones of Bosnian Muslim men and boys killed by Bosnian Serb forces.

Catching a Criminal

The United Nations International Criminal Tribunal for the Former Yugoslavia (ICTY) and Serbia and Montenegro declared Lukic a wanted man for his war crimes. The ICTY began to work with the Interpol General Secretariat and the Interpol NCBs in Argentina and Chile to bring Lukic to justice. Interpol issued a red notice against him. Lukic was using a false name and had a false passport, but when Argentinean authorities captured him, the Interpol NCB in Buenos Aires was able to confirm that the prisoner was Lukic by sending his fingerprints for immediate comparison. Lukic was arrested in Buenos Aires on August 7, 2005, and was sentenced to life imprisonment for six separate incidents of war crimes.

Inside Interpol

Working for Interpol requires a great deal of patience and determination. In the case of Milan Lukic, it took almost 20 years to see the war criminal brought to justice. This would not have been possible without the persistent work of those working in Interpol NCBs.

Bosnian Serbs committed mass murder against Bosnian Muslims in the town and district of Višegrad during 1992.

The Madrid Train Bombings

On March 11, 2004, a series of bombs exploded within minutes of each other on four commuter trains in Madrid, the capital city of Spain. The blasts killed 191 people and wounded nearly 2,000 more. A Moroccan terrorist group, Moroccan Islamist Combat Group (GICM), became the focus in the investigation. Through the work of Interpol, some arrests were made, but other suspects died in an explosion when Spanish police closed in on an apartment in Madrid in April 2004.

Some of the terrorists behind the Madrid train bombings died in an explosion in this building in 2004.

Red Notice

Investigations showed another Moroccan man, Abdelmajid Bouchar, was a suspect in the bombings. After an arrest warrant was put out for Bouchar in May 2004, the General Secretariat of Interpol issued a red notice on him. The search was on. Bouchar's details were distributed around Interpol NCBs, and law enforcement agencies and border controls were on constant lookout for him.

Fingerprinted!

In the end, Bouchar was stopped and held by police in Serbia after he failed to produce identification papers. He told the police he was an Iraqi named Midhat Salah; however, messages between NCB Belgrade and NCB Baghdad proved this was a lie. Officers in Belgrade sent his photograph and fingerprints to NCBs around the world using I-24/7. In no time, Interpol officers at the NCB in Madrid were able to make a positive match on the Interpol database, proving he was indeed Bouchar. With this evidence, the Serbian police were able to arrest him immediately.

Fingerprint Files

Interpol manages a database of fingerprints that contains more than 181,000 fingerprint records and almost 11,000 latent fingerprints. In 2017, the organization made more than 2,000 identifications as a result of data sharing and comparison by member countries.

These messages and flowers were left in memory of those killed in the Madrid train bombings in 2004.

The Simda Botnet

The word "botnet" is formed from the words "robot" and "network." A botnet is malware that cybercriminals use to take over a number of other people's computers. The botnet organizes all of the infected computers into a network of Internet-connected "bots" that the criminals can control from their own computers. In 2015, the Simda botnet was believed to have infected more than 770,000 computers in more than 190 countries worldwide. It was used by cybercriminals to gain remote access to computers, enabling the theft of personal details, including banking passwords, as well as to install and spread other malware.

The operation to bring down the Simda botnet was spearheaded by Interpol, which worked with and coordinated the efforts of other major organizations.

Taking Down the Simda Botnet

The Interpol Digital Crime Centre (IDCC) at the IGCI in Singapore worked with other organizations, including computer and technology company Microsoft and Japan's Cyber Defense Institute, to target the Simda botnet and bring it down. Organizations supplied forensic intelligence to Interpol for analysis. Using its analysis of the data, Interpol was able to produce a heat map that showed the spread of the infections globally and the location of the servers that were being used to control the infected systems. Using this information, the IGCI was able to organize its colleagues to perform a simultaneous takedown of the command and control servers around the world.

Using Stolen Data

Many botnets are designed to gather personal data, such as passwords, credit card information, addresses, and telephone numbers. Criminals can use the data in crimes such as identity theft (for example, using another person's name and personal information in order to obtain bank loans), various types of fraud, spamming (sending electronic junk mail), and malware distribution. Botnets can also be used to launch attacks on websites and networks. Interpol advises that all computer users should have antivirus software installed and make sure it is updated regularly.

The Simda botnet affected many countries, but the United States, UK, Turkey, Canada, and Russia were hit worst.

CHAPTER 6

A COVERT CAREER

Interpol does a vitally important job helping other law enforcement agencies around the world track criminals who operate across national borders. When people work for Interpol, they belong to the only police organization that spans the entire globe—so, how do they land this covert role?

Interpol Staff

The General Secretariat at Interpol employs about 800 people. Staff are based at the main secretariat building in Lyon, France, the IGCI in Singapore, or in the NCBs around the world. About one-third of Interpol staff is seconded to the organization. This means that they are law enforcement officers or officials who are transferred from their regular organization for temporary assignments working for Interpol in one of its 192 member countries. The other two-thirds of Interpol staff are international civil servants. That means they are administrative staff who help run the organization and are hired directly by Interpol.

Learning languages is good for most careers, but for many Interpol officers, it is essential.

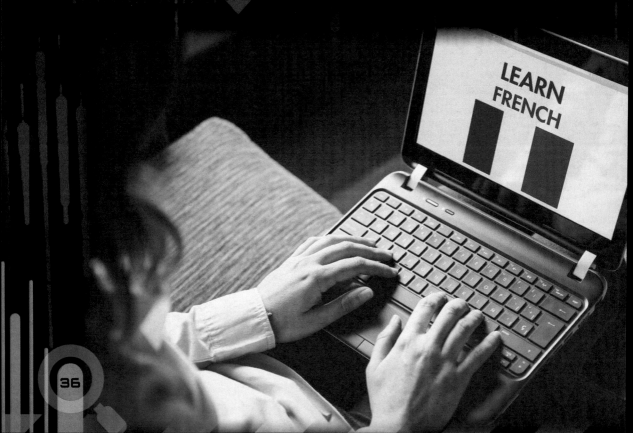

LEARN FRENCH

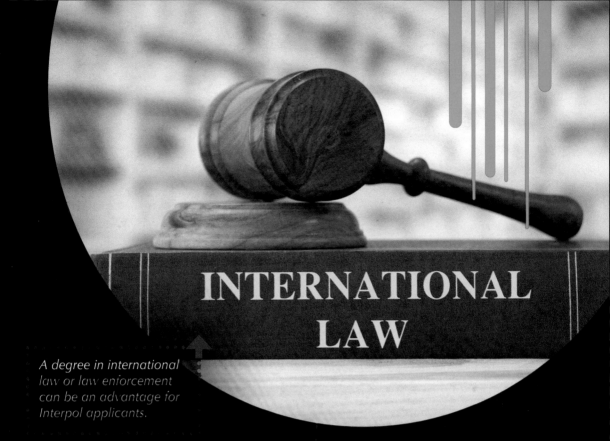

A degree in international law or law enforcement can be an advantage for Interpol applicants.

Education and Qualifications

To secure a job in either a seconded position or as a civil servant, it is important to get good grades and be someone who studies hard at school. A graduate degree with a specialty in international law and crime can make you a better candidate for Interpol. It can also help if applicants get a relevant degree in international law enforcement. Having a good knowledge of more than one of the Interpol official languages—Arabic, French, English, and Spanish—will also be considered an advantage, so taking language classes at school and possibly at the college level, or through private lessons, will be useful.

Inside Interpol

Interpol demands high standards from its staff. Interpol states that its staff values are respect, integrity, excellence, teamwork, and innovation. The actions of international officials should be guided by these values, which they should reflect in their work and daily activities.

Applying for an Internship

Many of the people who work as civil servants for Interpol start off by joining one of Interpol's internships. To be eligible or able to apply for an internship, all applicants must:

- Be enrolled in, or have graduated from, a postsecondary accredited academic institution within the past six months of the date of submission of their application
- Be a national of one of Interpol's member countries
- Be a legal adult in their country of nationality
- Be fluent in English
- Meet the requirements for each internship they wish to apply for

Applicants should put time and effort into writing the best cover letter they can.

Application Paperwork

When applying for an internship, candidates have to complete an online application form and attach a cover letter that includes their motivation to join the Interpol internship program, their qualifications that suit the specific internship for which they are applying, and their expectations for the internship.

How Internships Work

Interns learn about criminal justice systems, issues affecting international criminal investigations, Interpol's goals and objectives, and how international police cooperation is organized. They also do practical work assignments and get training from active law enforcement officers to develop useful skills. When they are assigned to different divisions of Interpol, such as violent crimes, counterterrorism, or the fugitives division, the training they receive may be tailored to a specific area of activity and to the duty station where they work. For example, interns at the counterterrorism division might learn how to investigate leads about planned terrorist activities, and how to analyze and assess these threats and write reports about them. They will also learn how to pursue the international arrest of terrorists.

International Internships

Interpol accepts applications from nationals of all its member countries. This ensures that it truly represents all of the countries that make it an international organization and a world police force.

The length of an Interpol internship varies from a minimum of six to a maximum of eleven months.

Police cooperation is central to Interpol's missions, which is why Interpol employs people from member countries with law enforcement experience or who are seconded or placed on loan for a specified period or tour. For example, in the United States, Interpol seconds agents from agencies such as the FBI, New York Police Department, the National Sheriff's Association, and other state, local, and federal law enforcement agencies. Initial secondments are normally for a period of three years, but the Secretary General may extend the secondment to up to six years.

Seconded Officials

For a law enforcement agent to be able to work for Interpol, they must make a request via their chain of command. They discuss their interest in handling Interpol-related cases with their commanding officer and ask if they can get experience working on cases and issues that are dispatched to federal, state, and local agencies by Interpol. They can also contact their local NCB to express their interest in being more involved in international cases. It helps if officers can get positions in law enforcement agencies that have higher volumes of Interpol cases, such as the FBI, because they are more likely to work on Interpol cases than local police officers.

Some FBI agents are seconded to Interpol to work on cases.

All Interpol officers must have security clearance to be able to review Interpol files.

Security Clearance

Anyone who works for Interpol must be security cleared. To gain security clearance, a person must undergo a process of examination and evaluation involving a background check, before employment is offered to them. Background checks find out if a person, for example, has a police record, has ever been in financial trouble, or has ever taken illegal drugs. Security clearance is needed for Interpol to protect against threats from hostile intelligence services, cybersecurity threats, terrorists, and other pressure groups. The results of the background checks determine who can be given access to sensitive information.

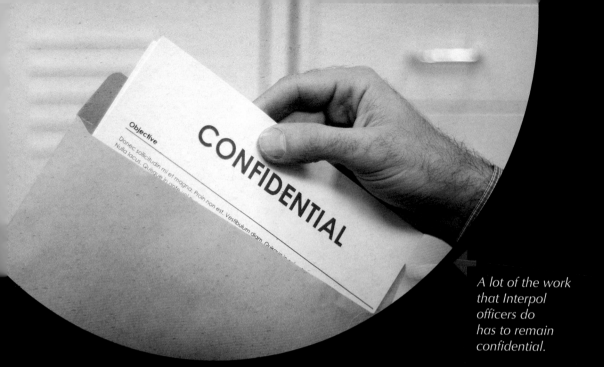

Objective

Donec sollicitudin mi et magna. Proin non est. Vestibulum diam. Quisque in ante.
Nulla lacus. Quisque in ante.

CONFIDENTIAL

*A lot of the work
that Interpol
officers do
has to remain
confidential.*

Joining Interpol

People who join Interpol are not in it for the glory. They are not the police
officers who are on the front line chasing bad guys like they do in movies
or in media broadcasts arresting notorious criminals. They do not break
down doors or risk being shot by a fugitive. There is no Interpol jail where
criminals are taken. However, without the people who work for Interpol,
the law enforcement officers who arrest international criminals might
not have caught them in the first place. People who work for Interpol are
proud to provide an international support system that helps crime fighters
around the world.

A Job That Matters

The people who work for Interpol have a great deal of knowledge and
access to information about international crime, so they are expected to
be discreet and keep any and all information they gather confidential
until it is published. When people work for Interpol, they must also be
prepared to travel to any part of the world at short notice for assignments
that may last for quite a long time. They must also be prepared to
work day and night shifts, on weekdays and on weekends, and on
public holidays. People who work for Interpol must be dedicated and
professional. After all, they help law enforcement agents around the
world see the big picture of international crime.

Other International Agencies

Interpol is not the only international law enforcement agency in the world. Europol works in a similar way to Interpol but only within the European Union. The United Nations Police consists of about 13,000 UN police officers. These officers are active members of their home police services from 90 countries around the world, but they are seconded to work with the UN.

Interpol works with other police agencies, such as Europol, to stop international crime.

A COVERT CAREER WITH INTERPOL

Would you like a career with Interpol? Following these steps will help set you on your path.

At School

You do not need to study particular subjects, but math, science, psychology, languages, and technology will be useful. Take opportunities to mix and deal with people from a wide range of backgrounds, and be aware of international news and politics.

At College

For most jobs with Interpol, you will need to have completed a college course and attained a relevant degree or diploma, for example, in international law or law enforcement. Having good knowledge of more than one of the Interpol official languages helps, too.

Background Checks

Everyone who applies to join Interpol undergoes a background investigation to check if they have ever taken illegal drugs, been in financial trouble, or have a police record.

Age Requirements

When they apply for a job, Interpol candidates must be the age legally defined as adult in their country of nationality.

Successful Applicants

Internships: To work as a civil servant for Interpol, candidates must complete an internship. To apply for an internship, applicants must be enrolled in, or have graduated from, a postsecondary accredited academic institution within the past six months on the date of submission of their application and be a national of one of Interpol's member countries.

Secondments: Law enforcement officials, such as FBI agents, who want to work for Interpol must make a request via their chain of command. If accepted, they will work for Interpol for three to six years.

Joining Interpol: When people officially succeed in joining Interpol, they begin working immediately in the Secretariat building in Lyon, France, the IGCI in Singapore, or one of the regional offices or NCBs.

GLOSSARY

background check An investigation into a person's past activities—including checks to find out if they have been involved in any crimes.

civil servants People employed in the public sector for a government department or agency.

corruption Illegal and dishonest behavior by people in business or politics for their own personal gain, for example, taking bribes.

counterterrorism Activities designed to prevent terrorism.

database A collection of information held on a computer that is organized so that it can be easily accessed, managed, and updated.

demographics The number and characteristics of people who live in a particular area.

DNA The chemical code found in every cell of the human body that makes each of us unique.

doping Taking drugs to improve athletic performance.

ethnic Relating to races or large groups of people who have the same customs, religion, or origins.

extradition Making someone return for trial to another country or state where they have been accused.

human rights Rights that are believed to belong to every person.

innovation New ideas or ways of doing something.

internships Periods of work experience offered by an organization for a limited period of time.

latent fingerprints Fingerprints invisible to the naked eye.

malware Software that is specifically designed to disrupt, damage, or gain authorized access to a computer system.

money laundering The methods criminals use to make it appear as if money obtained from criminal activity was made legally.

prosecute To officially accuse someone of committing a crime in a court of law.

sanctions Official orders, such as the stopping of trade, that are made against a country in order to make it obey international law.

satellite A machine placed in orbit around the earth to collect information or for communication.

seconded Transferred from one's regular organization or place of work to a temporary assignment or job elsewhere.

telegraphic Sent by telegraph, an old form of communication.

trafficking Dealing or trading in something illegal.

United Nations (UN) An international organization formed to promote international peace, security, and cooperation.

FOR MORE INFORMATION

BOOKS

Evans, Colin. *Law Enforcement Agencies: Interpol*. New York, NY: Chelsea House Publishing, 2011.

Gray, Leon. *Crime Science: Cybercrime*. New York, NY: Gareth Stevens, 2013.

Johnson, C. M. *Origins: Whodunnit: Organized Crime*. Minneapolis, MN: Full Tilt Press, 2017.

Latta, Sarah L., and Angie Timmons. *Crime Scene Investigators: Investigating Cybercrime*. Berkeley Heights, NJ: Enslow Publishing, 2018.

WEBSITES

Discover more about Interpol jobs at:
www.interpol.int/Recruitment

Find answers to many questions about Interpol at:
www.interpol.int/FAQs

Find out more about how Interpol works at:
people.howstuffworks.com/interpol.htm

Check out details about Interpol's history and more at:
www.britannica.com/topic/Interpol

INDEX